Hark! The herald angels
sing

Carols for Christmas

Hark! The Herald Angels Sing

Music arranged by Barrie Carson Turner

THE NATIONAL GALLERY, LONDON

Frances Lincoln
in association with
National Gallery Publications, London

Angels, from the Realms of Glory

French traditional

3. Sages, leave your contemplations;
   Brighter visions beam afar;
   Seek the great Desire of Nations;
   Ye have seen his natal star:
   Come and worship...

4. Though an infant now we view him,
   He shall fill his Father's throne,
   Gather all the nations round him,
   Every knee shall then bow down:
   Come and worship...

In the Bleak Midwinter

Gustav Holst (1874-1934)
Words by Christina Georgina Rossetti
(1830-94)

Moderately

1. In the bleak mid - win - ter   Frost - y wind made moan,
2. God, heaven can - not hold him   Nor ___ earth sus - tain;

Earth stood hard as   ir - on,   Wa - ter like a   stone;
Heaven and earth shall   flee a - way   When he comes to   reign:

Snow had fall - en,   snow on snow,   snow ___ on ___ snow,
In the bleak mid - win - ter   sta - ble place suf - ficed

In the bleak mid - win - ter,   Long ___ a - go.   2. Our
The Lord God Al - might - y,   Je - - - sus Christ.

3. Angels and archangels
    May have gathered there,
    Cherubim and seraphim
    Thronged the air;
    But only his mother
    In her maiden bliss
    Worshipped the Belovèd
    With a kiss.

4. What can I give him,
    Poor as I am?
    If I were a shepherd
    I would bring a lamb;
    If I were a wise man
    I would do my part
    Yet what I can I give him –
    Give my heart.

The First Nowell

English melody arr. John Stainer (1840-1901)
Words traditional

3. And by the light of that same star,
   Three Wise Men came from country far;
   To seek for a king was their intent,
   And to follow the star wherever it went:
       Nowell, Nowell, Nowell, Nowell…

4. This star drew nigh unto the north-west;
   O'er Bethlehem it took its rest,
   And there it did both stop and stay,
   Right over the place where Jesus lay:
       Nowell, Nowell, Nowell, Nowell…

5. Then entered in those Wise Men three,
   Fell reverently upon their knee,
   And offered there, in his presence,
   Their gold and myrrh and frankincense:
       Nowell, Nowell, Nowell, Nowell…

6. Then let us all with one accord
   Sing praises to our heavenly Lord,
   That hath made heaven and earth of nought,
   And with his blood mankind hath bought:
       Nowell, Nowell, Nowell, Nowell…

Silent Night

Franz Grüber (1787-1863)
Original German words by
Joseph Mohr (1792-1848)
Translation anon.

1. Si - lent night, ho - ly night, All is calm, all is bright,
Round yon vir - gin moth - er and child, Ho - ly in - fant so ten - der and mild,
Sleep in heav - en - ly peace, _____ Sleep __ in heav - en - ly peace.

2. Silent night, holy night,
   Shepherds first saw the light,
   Heard resounding clear and long,
   Far and near, the angel song:
   Christ the Saviour is here,
   Christ the Saviour is here.

3. Silent night, holy night,
   Son of God, oh, how bright
   Love is smiling from thy face,
   Peals for us the hour of grace.
   Christ our Saviour is born,
   Christ our Saviour is born.

O Come, All Ye Faithful

John Francis Wade (1711-86)
Words 18th century

3. Sing, choirs of angels,
   Sing in exultation.
   Sing, all ye citizens of heaven above;
   Glory to God
   In the highest:
   O come, let us adore him…

4. Yea, Lord, we greet thee,
   Born this happy morning,
   Jesu, to thee be glory given;
   Word of the Father,
   Now in flesh appearing:
   O come, let us adore him…

The Holly and the Ivy

English traditional

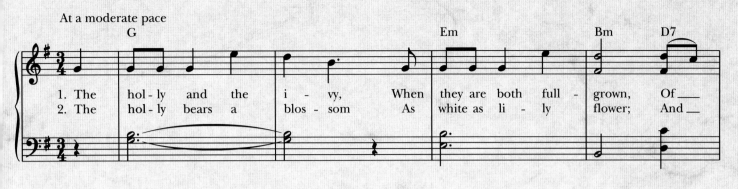

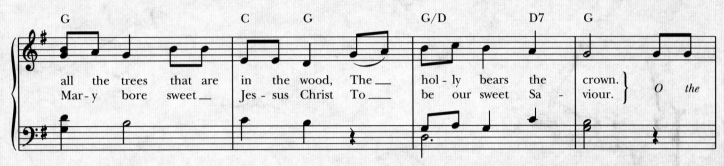

3. The holly bears a berry,
    As red as any blood;
    And Mary bore sweet Jesus Christ
    To do poor sinners good.
        O the rising of the sun…

4. The holly bears a prickle,
    As sharp as any thorn;
    And Mary bore sweet Jesus Christ
    On Christmas Day in the morn.
        O the rising of the sun…

5. The holly bears a bark,
    As bitter as any gall;
    And Mary bore sweet Jesus Christ,
    For to redeem us all.
        O the rising of the sun…

Hark! The Herald Angels Sing

Felix Mendelssohn (1809-47)
*from **Festgesang** (1840)*

Moderately fast

1. Hark! The her - ald an - gels sing ___ Glor - y to the new - born King;
2. Christ, by high - est heaven a - dored, ___ Christ, the ev - er - last - ing Lord;

Peace on earth, and mer - cy mild, ___ God and sin - ners re - con - ciled.
Late in time be - hold him come, ___ Off - spring of a Vir - gin's womb.

Joy - ful, all you na - tions, rise, ___ Join the tri - umph of the skies; ___
Veiled in flesh the God - head see; ___ Hail, the In - car - nate De - i - ty, ___

With the an-gel - lic hosts pro - claim, Christ is ___ born in Beth - le - hem.
Pleased as man with man to dwell, Je - sus, ___ our Em- man - u - el!

Hark! The her - ald an - gels sing, Glo - ry ___ to the new - born King.

3. Hail the heaven-born Prince of Peace!
   Hail the Sun of Righteousness!
   Light and life to all he brings,
   Risen with healing in his wings.
   Mild he lays his glory by,
   Born that man no more may die,
   Born to raise the sons of earth,
   Born to give them second birth.
       Hark! The herald angels sing,
       Glory to the new-born King.

Once in Royal David's City

Henry John Gauntlett (1805-76)
Words by Cecil Frances Alexander
(1818-95)

3. And through all his wondrous childhood
   He would honour and obey,
   Love and watch the lowly maiden,
   In whose gentle arms he lay.
   Christian children all must be
   Mild, obedient, good as he.

4. And our eyes at last shall see him,
   Through his own redeeming love,
   For that child so dear and gentle
   Is our Lord in heaven above;
   And he leads his children on
   To the place where he is gone.

God Rest You Merry, Gentlemen

English traditional

3. 'Fear not,' then said the Angel,
   'Let nothing you affright,
   This day is born a Saviour
   Of virtue, power and might;
   So frequently to vanquish all
   The friends of Satan quite':
       O tidings of comfort and joy…

4. The shepherds at these tidings,
   Rejoicèd much in mind,
   And left their flocks a-feeding
   In tempest, storm, and wind,
   And went to Bethlehem straightway
   This blessèd babe to find:
       O tidings of comfort and joy…

5. And when they came to Bethlehem
   Where our sweet Saviour lay,
   They found him in a manger,
   Where oxen feed on hay;
   His mother Mary kneeling,
   Unto the Lord did pray:
       O tidings of comfort and joy…

6. Now to the Lord sing praises,
   All you within this place,
   And with true love and brotherhood
   Each other now embrace;
   This holy tide of Christmas
   All others doth deface:
       O tidings of comfort and joy…

O Little Town of Bethlehem

English traditional

3. How silently, how silently,
The wondrous gift is given!
So God imparts to human hearts
The blessings of his heaven.
No ear may hear his coming;
But in this world of sin,
Where meek souls will receive him, still
The dear Christ enters in.

4. O holy Child of Bethlehem,
Descend to us, we pray;
Cast out our sin, and enter in,
Be born in us today.
We hear the Christmas angels
The great glad tidings tell:
O come to us, abide with us,
Our Lord Emmanuel.

See Amid the Winter's Snow

John Goss (1800-1880)
Words by Edward Caswall
(1814-78)

3. Say, ye holy shepherds, say,
   What your joyful news today;
   Wherefore have ye left your sheep
   On the lonely mountain steep?
   Hail! thou ever-blessèd morn…

4. 'As we watched at dead of night,
   Lo, we saw a wondrous light;
   Angels singing "Peace on Earth",
   Told us of the Saviour's birth.'
   Hail! thou ever-blessèd morn…

5. Sacred Infant, all divine,
   What a tender love was thine;
   Thus to come from highest bliss
   Down to such a world as this!
   Hail! thou ever-blessèd morn…

6. Teach, O teach us, Holy Child,
   By thy face so meek and mild;
   Teach us to resemble thee
   In thy sweet humility.
   Hail! thou ever-blessèd morn…

Good King Wenceslas

*Melody from **Piae Cantiones** (1582)*
Words by J. M. Neale (1818-66)

3. 'Bring me flesh and bring me wine,
   Bring me pine-logs hither:
   Thou and I will see him dine
   When we bear them thither.'
   Page and monarch, forth they went,
   Forth they went together;
   Through the rude wind's wild lament
   And the bitter weather.

4. 'Sire, the night is darker now,
   And the wind grows stronger;
   Fails my heart, I know not how;
   I can go no longer.'
   'Mark my footsteps, good my page;
   Tread thou in them boldly:
   Thou shalt find the winter's rage
   Freeze thy blood less coldly.'

5. In his master's steps he trod,
   Where the snow lay dinted;
   Heat was in the very sod
   Which the Saint had printed.
   Therefore, Christian men, be sure,
   Wealth or rank possessing,
   Ye who now will bless the poor,
   Shall yourselves find blessing.

Away in a Manger

William James Kirkpatrick (1838-1921)
Words anon.

2. The cattle are lowing, the baby awakes,
   But little Lord Jesus, no crying he makes.
   I love thee, Lord Jesus! Look down from the sky,
   And stay by my side until morning is nigh.

3. Be near me, Lord Jesus; I ask thee to stay
   Close by me for ever, and love me, I pray.
   Bless all the dear children in thy tender care,
   And fit us for heaven, to live with thee there.

While Shepherds Watched

*Este's **Psalmes** (1592)*

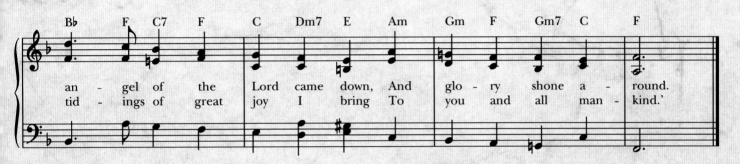

3. 'To you in David's town this day
    Is born of David's line
    A Saviour, who is Christ the Lord;
    And this shall be the sign:

4. 'The heavenly Babe you there shall find
    To human view displayed,
    All meanly wrapped in swaddling bands,
    And in a manger laid.'

5. Thus spake the seraph; and forthwith
    Appeared a shining throng
    Of angels praising God, who thus
    Addressed their joyful song:

6. 'All glory be to God on high,
    And to the earth be peace;
    Goodwill henceforth from heaven to men
    Begin and never cease!'

We Three Kings

Words and music by
John Henry Hopkins (1820-91)

Smooth and flowing

1. We three Kings of O - ri - ent are; Bear - ing gifts we trav - erse a - far,
2. Born a King on Beth - le - hem plain, Gold I bring, to crown him a - gain,

Field and foun - tain, moor and moun - tain, Fol - low - ing yon - der star:
King for - ev - er, ceas - ing nev - er, Ov - er us all to reign: } O ____

star of won - der, star of night, Star with roy - al beau - ty bright,

West - ward lead - ing, still pro - ceed - ing, Guide us to thy per - fect light.

3. Frankincense to offer have I,
   Incense owns a Deity nigh;
   Prayer and praising, all men raising,
   Worship him, God most high:
       O star of wonder, star of night…

4. Myrrh is mine, its bitter perfume
   Breathes a life of gathering gloom;
   Sorrowing, sighing, bleeding, dying,
   Sealed in the stone-cold tomb:
       O star of wonder, star of night…

5. Glorious now behold him arise,
   King and God and sacrifice!
   Heaven sings alleluia,
   Alleluia the earth replies:
       O star of wonder, star of night…

Deck the Hall

Welsh traditional

1. Deck the hall with boughs of hol - ly,
   See the blaz - ing Yule be - fore us,
   Fa la la la la, la la la la,

'Tis the sea - son to be jol - ly,
Strike the harp and join the chor - us,
Fa la la la la, la la la la,

Don we now our gay ap - pa - rel,
Fol - low me in mer - ry mea - sure,
Fa la la, la la la, la la la,

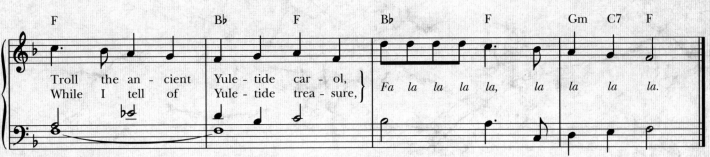

Troll the an - cient Yule - tide car - ol,
While I tell of Yule - tide trea - sure,
Fa la la la la, la la la la.

3.	Fast away the old year passes,
	Fa la la la la, la la la la,
	Hail the new, ye lads and lasses,
	Fa la la la la, la la la la,
	Sing we joyous all together,
	Fa la la, la la la, la la la,
	Heedless of the wind and weather,
	Fa la la la la, la la la la.

O Christmas Tree

German traditional

2. O Christmas tree, O Christmas tree!
Thou hast a wondrous message.
O Christmas tree, O Christmas tree!
Thou hast a wondrous message.
Thou dost proclaim the Saviour's birth,
Goodwill to men and peace on earth.
O Christmas tree, O Christmas tree!
Thou hast a wondrous message.

We Wish You a Merry Christmas

West Country traditional

2.   We all want some figgy pudding,
      We all want some figgy pudding,
      We all want some figgy pudding,
      So bring some out here!
        Good tidings we bring…

3.   We won't go until we get some,
      We won't go until we get some,
      We won't go until we get some,
      So bring some right here!
        Good tidings we bring…

Index

The illustrations are details of the following paintings.

Page 11
The Nativity and the Annunciation
Jacopo di Cione
(active about 1362; died 1398/1400)
This is the first of a series of panels showing the life of Christ. Here the artist combines two scenes: above, the angel announces the birth of Christ to two astonished shepherds, while below is the scene of the Nativity.

Page 13
The Nativity, at Night
Ascribed to Geertgen tot Sint Jans
(around 1455/65-85/95)
Geertgen's use of dramatic light was exceptional for his time. Here the night is lit both by the Infant and by the angel in the background who casts light over the shepherd and flock.

Page 15
'Mystic Nativity'
Sandro Botticelli
(active by 1470-1510)
In Botticelli's unconventional treatment of the subject, the Virgin is larger than the other figures. Angels broadcast the news of Christ's coming and the prospect of Peace on Earth; the devils scatter.

Page 17
The Virgin and Child in a Landscape
Attributed to Jan Provoost
(living 1491; died 1529)
The mother and child sit in the countryside, surrounded by plants and flowers. Jesus is playing with a whirligig, a toy with a spinning top. To his left is a pot of carnations, which was probably used to symbolize his suffering and his death on the Cross.

Pages 18 and 19
Christ Glorified in Heaven
Fra Angelico
(active 1417; died 1455)
See the entry for the cover and jacket flaps.

Page 20
The Adoration of the Kings
Jan Brueghel the Elder
(1568-1625)
Brueghel's paintings are full of lively detail, such as the crowd of onlookers in the foreground of this painting, the figures on the bank of the river in the background and Joseph's woodworking tools in the lower right corner.

Page 23

Seraphim, Cherubim and Adoring Angels
Jacopo di Cione
(active about 1362; died 1398/1400)
This was one of two panels of adoring angels that formed part of the altarpiece of a church in Florence (see *The Nativity and the Annunciation*, page 11).

Page 24

The Rest on the Flight into Egypt
Master of the Female Half-Lengths
(16th century)
The Holy Family is shown resting and refreshing themselves on their journey into Egypt to escape Herod. In the background, a man is at work in the field of corn that grew miraculously overnight to mislead Herod's soldiers.

Page 27

A Scene on the Ice near a Town
Hendrick Avercamp
(1585-1634)
The figures skating, riding in hand-drawn sleighs, and playing *Kolf* (an early version of golf) on the frozen river could be from drawings and sketches made from life, although the town may be imaginary.

Page 29

A Winter Scene
Isack van Ostade
(1621-49)
The details of the frozen landscape and of the figures going about their daily lives highlight the effects of winter in the countryside. The man struggling over the bridge with his firewood, and the man guiding his horse and sleigh onto the bank are contrasted with the pleasure of the child who is waiting to go on the ice.

Page 31

The Adoration of the Shepherds
Louis (?) le Nain
(about 1593-1648)
Le Nain painted many pictures of ordinary country people. Here, the barefoot man kneeling with his back to us is a shepherd. The angels look like peasant children, with their tousled hair and curious glances.

Page 32

The Adoration of the Shepherds
Nicolas Poussin
(about 1594-1665)
In this painting the Christian
scene of the adoration contains
many classical allusions in the
ruins behind the Holy Family and
the style of dress of the figures.
The ruins and the new-born child
symbolize the ending of an era
with the birth of Christ.

Page 34

The Adoration of the Magi
Carlo Dolci
(1616-86)
One of the most famous painters
of his day, Dolci painted many
religious pictures. Here the three
richly dressed kings kneel before
Mary in the dark stable to offer
their gifts to Jesus.

Page 36

*Peasants Merry-making Before a
Country House*
Lucas van Uden (1595-1672)
and David Teniers the Younger
(1610-90)
Both the painters lived in
Antwerp and worked together on
a number of paintings. The
landscape was painted by van
Uden and the people merry-
making in the foreground by
David Teniers, who is well known
for his scenes of country life.

Page 38

A Winter Landscape
Caspar David Friedrich
(1774-1840)
This German artist often painted
landscapes with a symbolic
meaning. Here the message is one
of hope: the man has thrown away
his crutches and sits against a rock
with his hands raised in prayer.

Page 41

A Concert
Lorenzo Costa
(1459/60-1535)
This was probably one of a series
of paintings of singers with
different musical instruments.
Artists in Costa's time were
interested in conveying the idea of
sound, in this case singing, and
demonstrating their skill in
showing expressions on people's
faces (see the angels in Piero della
Francesca's *Nativity*, page 9).

Hark! The Herald Angels Sing copyright
© Frances Lincoln Limited 1993
Picture index © Frances Lincoln Limited 1993
Music arrangements © Barrie Carson Turner, Burgate,
Diss, Norfolk, IP22 1QG

All illustrations are reproduced by courtesy of the Trustees,
The National Gallery, London.

First published in Great Britain in 1993 by
Frances Lincoln Limited, 4 Torriano Mews,
Torriano Avenue, London NW5 2RZ
www.franceslincoln.com

First paperback edition 2002

British Library Cataloguing in Publication Data
available on request

ISBN 0-7112-2069-7

Set in Baskerville
Printed and bound in Hong Kong

Designed by Patrica Howes

1 3 5 7 9 8 6 4 2

MORE PICTURE BOOKS FROM FRANCES LINCOLN

THE FIRST CHRISTMAS
Words from the King James Bible
Illustrated with paintings from the National Gallery

The beauty of the familiar words from the King James Bible weaves
these and other glorious images together to create a new work of art:
a Christmas story that will be treasured by readers young and old.

ISBN 0-7112-0784-4

BETHLEHEM
Words from the King James Bible
Illustrated by Fiona French

Inspired by England's glorious stained-glass cathedral windows
and using the magnificent words from the King James Bible,
the story of the first Christmas unfolds in a kaleidoscope
of colours and with breathtaking panoramas, illuminating
the story's miraculous events and timeless beauty.

ISBN 0-7112-1576-6

LIVES AND LEGENDS OF THE SAINTS
Carole Armstrong
Illustrated with paintings from
the great art museums of the world

Newly retold and celebrated in paintings by some of the world's
finest artists are the lives and legends of twenty well-loved saints.
An index of paintings and a calendar of feast-days help provide
an inspiring introduction to these heroic personalities.

ISBN 0-7112-1672-X

Frances Lincoln titles are available from all good bookshops.
You can also buy books and find out more about your favourite titles,
authors and illustrators at our website: www.franceslincoln.com.